I received _____ :er the initial distr. _____ .nother printing of it, I wanted to share portions of a few of them (some slightly edited for clarity).

~ *Comforting, inspiring, encouraging—all that and more.*

~ *God isn't as far away from me as I thought.*

~ *I never felt good enough, but this book helped me see how valuable I am to God.*

~ *This book caused me to look at my life and all the times God was there.*

~ *I found your book to be thought-provoking and contemplative.*

~ *I know that God's hand was with the boys and me during my husband's illness and death. It is important to continue to remember the ways He has walked with us.*

~ *I read your book in two days—couldn't put it down.*

~ *I shall surely share this book with those who need a jolt of positivity, a source of inspiration and a wonderful reminder of God's power and its reflection in their lives.*

~ *I am going to share parts of your book when I teach Sunday School.*

~ *This book made me reflect on my life story and realize how God and His angels intersected it.*

~ Reading this book is so powerful and brings even more gratitude for how great our God is!

~ I would like ten copies of your book for my family. I have had a near-death experience. "Next thing I knew, I passed out and died ... It was so peaceful."

~ It empowered us to be bolder in sharing our stories of when God has spoken to us.

~ I plan to use this book as a personal study guide.

~ I would love to be able to share your book with family.

~ I am giving one of your books to a friend of mine and another to a friend who lost his wife this year in an auto accident.

~ I thoroughly enjoyed the examples you used in the front part of the book that appeared to be derived from your personal experience, the Bible and from your counseling experience.

~ This book is a wonderful witness of the power of God's love and how you saw it work in your ministry.

It is my prayer that this book will also be helpful to you and those you love.

Stan Murdoch
July 2023

GOD IS POWERFUL...

AND THERE IS SOMETHING HE HAS FOR YOU TO DO

(Expanded Edition)

Life Experiences, Reflections and Insights
Supporting the Truths of Scripture

*May these personal stories
of experiences with God
inspire you and those you love.*

STS

Stanley C. Murdoch

(THIS BOOK IS FREE. See Page 99 for details.)

God is Powerful...
And There is Something
He Has For You to Do

Copyright © 2022
Expanded Edition Copyright © 2023
Stanley C. Murdoch

Cover design selection and layout by Pam Murdoch.

Photo of author on back cover ©Artisans Photography of Kearney, Nebraska. Used by permission.

Initial Printing ISBN 979-8-218-09417-1
Expanded Edition ISBN 979-8-218-23623-6

FOR INFORMATION CONTACT:

murdochstan51@gmail.com

Printed in the USA by
Morris Publishing®
3212 E. Hwy. 30 · Kearney, NE 68847
800-650-7888 · www.morrispublishing.com

THIS BOOK IS DEDICATED TO:

- My family, especially my dear wife, Pam, who has walked with me on this journey and to our dear children and their families: our son, Nathan, and his wife, Tiffany, and their children Bennett, Maxwell, Evelyn and Rutheah; our daughter, Emily, and her husband, Kellen, and their children Teyah, Oakleigh, Quinten and Lilah Faithe.

- All the pastors who faithfully guide and care for the Church, the Body of Christ. You have such a rewarding and challenging calling from the Lord.

- The many people referred to in Chapter Six (*What Do You See?*). You have heard God's voice of acceptance, forgiveness and grace and are now following the Lord.

THIS BOOK IS WRITTEN with gratitude for—and with fond memories of—the pastors and Christians who have gone before me. I am especially thankful for those mentioned in Chapter Seven (*On Death Beds*). It was their experiences at death that continued to teach me about the power and love of God.

TABLE OF CONTENTS

(continued)

PREFACE

As I have undertaken the task of writing the following in 2022, it is fair to ask the question, "Why are you writing?" There are several reasons.

1. Initially, I was only going to write about my drowning experience with God. The first time I wrote about that experience was just in note form when I left home for college. I felt compelled to write that note so that if "something happened to me," my parents would know why I was studying to become a pastor. So, I wrote the note and left it in my safety box at home.

   I remember the phone call at college in the spring of the year after my folks found the note while doing my taxes. My mom said, "We found your note." There was silence on the phone until I finally responded, "Okay." Until that moment, they never knew why I was going into the ministry.

   Now I have written a full account of my drowning experience with God so others can know how greatly it impacted the rest of my life.

2. When I retired from the pastoral role of ministry, I was asked several times if I was going to do any writing. I always responded, "I don't know." It always seemed like there are plenty of people who have written so much. How could anything I write be important? Then I was reminded of the importance of telling one's own stories to encourage, inspire and teach those who follow us.

So, now I will write about some of my personal experiences with God.

3. It seems, to me, that there is a universal danger of people thinking that the God of the Bible stopped revealing Himself to people at the conclusion of the Bible. If anything, by reading the Bible, we should recognize that the God of the Bible does not change. Therefore, He continues to reveal Himself to more people than we can possibly imagine, just as He revealed Himself as recorded in the Bible. *If only we knew the stories!*

My hope is that what I write will encourage all ages — children, teens and adults. To help you in this regard, I have included a chapter-by-chapter Study Section at the end of the book. It is designed to be helpful for individual study and/or small group study.

God is powerful, and there is something He has for you to do!

May God Bless You,

Stan Murdoch

Chapter One

SEEING GOD'S HAND

The following is a detailed account of an experience I had at around age 10. This was an experience that I never told anyone about for many years. I was afraid to tell the following account because I was afraid of what people would think of me. It was finally in college, when I was asked, "Why are you studying to become a pastor?" that I told this account for the first time—the account of an experience about drowning and seeing God's hand.

Some may dismiss this story as unbelievable or made up. So be it, but I know I was drowning in a pool at about age 10. I know what I saw and heard in that experience. I know how this experience affected every aspect of my life from that day until now.

We were a family of our parents and five children. We were a hardworking family. We lived as a Christian family, going to church and Sunday School, but we had our share of hurts and troubles just like any other family. It was summertime in southern Nebraska and Mom signed us up for swimming lessons in the nearby town of Orleans. Many years before, Mom had a little brother drown in a flash flood in South Dakota. They never found his body. So, I assume her desire for us to have swimming lessons was very personal for her.

One of those mornings at swimming lessons, my swimming instructor, a young man about age 16, said to me, "We need to get you in deeper water so you can learn how to kick." I was a tall and skinny 10-year-old boy, so it made sense I needed deeper water to learn to kick.

As we got to the deep end of the pool, he told me to jump into the water and grab the edge of the pool. I jumped into the eight to nine feet of water, but my hands were too wet to grab the edge. The next thing I knew, I was down deep into the water and struggling. I remember struggling to grab onto anything. I remember the bubbles swirling around me. I remember the great fear that engulfed me.

Then, in this time of drowning in the depth of the swimming pool, I saw a huge hand. It was a right hand and was two to three feet long in my mind's eye. This hand cupped under me and gently lifted me up and out of the water. The next thing I knew I was sitting on the side of the pool. There was no one around me. My swimming instructor had evidently jumped in after me and was still in the water looking for me.

Shortly thereafter, his head popped up out of the water directly in front of me and he was gasping for air. Then he saw me sitting on the side of the pool and said, "Oh, here you are!" I remember feeling anger towards him because he had not helped me. So, I responded tersely, "Yes!" He then responded exhaustingly, "That's it for the day. Go change your clothes!"

He was still in the water when I started walking to the pool house. I had only taken a few steps when I heard a voice say to me, "God is powerful, and there is something He has for you to do!"

2

As I stated earlier, I never told anyone about this experience until many years later, when I was in college.

Why didn't I tell anyone this story? Because I was afraid people would make fun of me. Many years have gone by since that day, yet I think of that experience daily. I've also wrestled with questions about that experience.

1. Was it God's hand that I saw?
2. Was it God's voice that I heard?
3. What does God want me to do?
4. Why did this happen to me?

First, was it God's hand that I saw? *The hand was not human. It was two to three feet long.* It looked like a human hand but much bigger. How does God do something like this? I have wondered whether it was the hand of Jesus or of an angel. But another aspect of the hand became clearer to me as I began to learn more Scriptures (Exodus 15:6, Psalm 44:3, Psalm 63:8, Psalm 98:1, Psalm 110:1, Matthew 22:44, Matthew 26:64, Mark 16:19, Acts 7:55, Hebrews 1:13). The hand in the pool was a *right hand!*

I always remembered the right hand and its thumb, but it was not until I learned the Scriptures that I understood the importance of this detail. The Scriptures repeatedly use the phrase "right hand of God." The right hand of God can mean the closeness of God, the power of God or the authority of God. However God did this, I believe it was God's right hand that lifted me out of the depth of the water, and His right hand placed me securely on the side of the pool!

3

Second, was it God's voice that I heard? For many years, I believed that it was God's voice that I heard. It was only later in life that I began to look deeper at these very specific words: "God is powerful, and there is something He has for you to do!"

The very specific statement "God is powerful, and there is something He has for you to do!" has replayed almost every day of my life. So, upon deeper reflection of that very clear statement, said to a 10-year-old boy, I have come to believe this message was spoken to me by one of God's angels.

Angels are often referred to as messengers of God (Matthew 1:20, Luke 1:26, Luke 2:10, Acts 10:3-7). I remember this message so clearly. I have no question or wavering about what I heard. "God is powerful, and there is something He has for you to do!" I believe this message was from God, spoken through an angel to me, after being lifted up and out of the depths of a pool by the right hand of God.

Third, what did God want me to do? I started going to summer church camp as a boy. I experienced the many aspects of summer church camp: cabin life with a bunch of boys, the mess hall, Bible studies, outdoor activities and the campfires. I remember feeling so close to God at church camp. It was there that I began to ask God, "What do you want me to do?" I would say to God, "Whatever you want me to do, I will do." I didn't know what that would look like. Was it to become a missionary? Was it to become a pastor? Or, was it something else God wanted me to do?

The answer became clear to me in my high school years. As an active participant in my church youth group, I was asked to take roles of leadership and to attend youth conventions. But, most of all, it was at summer church camp that God touched my heart, my mind and my soul to convince me that I was to become a pastor.

After becoming a pastor, several older ladies of my hometown church told me they always knew I would become a pastor. I wondered why they said that since they didn't know about my drowning experience. When I finally did ask them how they knew I would become a pastor, they said, "It was because of how you listened during church. You leaned over the pew in front of you and listened intensely."

God had put a calling on my heart when I heard, "God is powerful, and there is something He has for you to do!" The older ladies of the church were watching me and discerned that calling. I was to become a pastor. This understanding was the beginning of a journey to discover what kind of pastor God wanted me to become.

Fourth, why did this happen to me? There is no question, for me, that this experience was God's doing. The drowning experience, the right hand and the voice that clearly said, "God is powerful, and there is something He has for you to do!" All of this has affected my life in such a way that I can never adequately express the significance of this experience on my life. But, in my 50s, I began to realize this experience and message was not just to me, but to anyone who will listen.

Let's look at the first part of the message: "God is powerful,"

> I was a boy frantically drowning in the bottom of the pool. I see a large, beyond human-size hand lift me up and set me on the edge of the pool. The voice explains that what just happened to me was from God. It is so important for us to come to know that God is powerful. Perhaps that is why it is so important for us to believe that Jesus is bodily risen to life from the dead. Believing that God is powerful is the beginning for us to understand God.

Let's look at the second part of the message: "and there is something He has for you to do!"

> Why would God need me? God can create the universe and all there is on this planet, yet God still wanted me to help do His work. This message transformed my search for the purpose of my life. When you know that Almighty God has a purpose for your life, it brings meaning to your life. You then begin to live your life as if it has eternal meaning. This to me is the most powerful part of the experience. The most powerful part is not being lifted from the pool. The most powerful part is that "there is something God has for you to do!"

So, why write this detailed account from an experience 60 years ago? Is this also a part of what God wanted me to do when He rescued me and spoke to me in that pool so many years ago? I know that I never could have guessed the wonderful journey He has had me on.

First, I have learned much more about God as I have pondered my experience.

- *God is not surprised by our difficulties.* When I went to swimming lessons that day, I did not know I would have a frightening drowning experience. But God did and His hand was already there to lift me up.

- *God knows people who feel insignificant.* If God can know a 10-year-old boy, in the middle of Nebraska, in the bottom of a pool, then God knows everyone who may feel insignificant.

- *God is always closer than we realize.* As a 10-year-old boy, I was just going to swimming lessons. I did not know that I would need God that day. But God knew I would need Him and He was already there.

- *God uses bad times to get our attention.* Could God have gotten my attention if I was just out for a walk? Yes, but not to the same extent. It often takes a "foxhole" experience for God to get our attention and for us to willingly listen to Him.

- *God brings the wonderful out of the horrible.* I would never want anyone to go through a drowning experience. But I would never exchange the wonderful good God brought to my life, through that horrible experience, for not seeing the power of God and His plan for my life.

7

- *God is powerful, but He still needs us.* God has created the universe and everything in it. But He still needs us to be a part of His ongoing acts of creation and restoration in this world.

Second, I have learned that stories can inspire others who need strength and encouragement. Stories of God and the people of the Bible have given strength and encouragement to all generations. Likewise, stories of the same God and people today can strengthen the weak and give courage to the weary.

- *God knew I would need this experience.* There were times in life and ministry that I would have given up except for the remembering of this experience. My strength was renewed in remembering this experience.

- *God gives us stories to help others.* We may not be the one drowning in the bottom of the pool, but we may be the one who is afraid and ready to give up. It is then that God, through my sharing of it, has given others the story to help them in their times of weakness and wandering.

- *God has given stories to many.* I have learned that God has also given experiences to more people than what we realize. But, just like me, they have been afraid to tell their story. The Bible tells us that God has been and is involved in the lives of young and old, men and women, saints and sinners. We just need to tell the story.

I have never written a detailed account of this story until now, 60 years later. I can never forget what happened or what was said to me. This was the beginning of seeing God's hand at various times in my life and ministry. I have more to write...

(See pages 76-77 for additional personal and/or group study of Chapter One.)

GOD IS POWERFUL

Chapter Two

LEARNING TO WATCH FOR GOD

The drowning experience, at age 10, opened my eyes to the God who interjects Himself into the lives of people. I cannot say that I was looking for God to appear. I can say I recognized when God did appear.

+   +   +   +   +   +   +

Looking back, before the drowning experience, I was in second grade, so about age 7 or 8, and I was sick a lot. The teachers had told my parents that if I missed any more days of school, they would have to hold me back. I remember how this frightened me.

First, I was not pretending to be sick. I had side aches on the right side of my abdomen, but the doctors could not find any reason for them.

Second, now I am in danger of being held back because I am sick and missing school. I remember crying and praying about how this seemed so unfair. I cried to God as a 7- or 8-year-old child, "Please don't let them hold me back in school."

I don't know what happened, except I no longer had side aches on the right side of my abdomen. But, I do know I have a round scar the size of a dime on the right side of my abdomen. That scar appeared when I was a child and is still there today.

+   +   +   +   +   +   +

At the age of 13 or 14, Dad had asked my brother and I to burn the dead weeds, corn husks and other debris that had blown into the ditch up the hill from our house. It was the spring of the year, when the seasons begin to change in southern Nebraska.

We had completed the task; the fires were out and we went home to have supper. Our house had a south-facing picture window near the dinner table; and, as Mom and us kids were having supper, we looked up to see the southwest sky orange with fire. A strong north wind had come up and evidently blown hot embers into the pasture across the road from the ditch we had cleaned out by burning. Mom called the town fire department while my brother and I ran up the hill with dirt shovels to try to put out the fire.

As we ran up the hill, it seemed that the whole sky was ablaze. I remember praying, "God, please help us." It seemed to be an overwhelming catastrophe. We started running in the pasture, with our shovels, trying to put out the fire that was now moving quickly in the short buffalo grass because of the strong wind. "God, please help us," I prayed repeatedly.

The next thing I knew, some small clouds from the west blew overhead dropping a small rain shower. By the time the fire trucks arrived, the fire in the pasture was out. The fire trucks then went around to cow pies to put water on anything still smoldering.

+   +   +   +   +   +   +

Another time, as a teenager, I was coming home from a date or school activity about midnight. I was driving on a gravel road near our home, going plenty fast, trying to get home, when I saw a black angus cow standing sideways right in the middle of the gravel road. For those that know gravel roads in Nebraska, you know they are just wide enough for two vehicles to meet and pass each other *if* you slow down because there is a pile of gravel on the edge of the road that can throw you off the road.

It was midnight and as dark out as that black angus cow. I had only a moment to whisper a prayer, "Help me," and to turn the steering wheel just enough without even braking.

The next thing I knew, I was past the angus cow, still standing sideways in the middle of the gravel road, and on my way home.

+   +   +   +   +   +   +

It was my first year of college. My twin sister and I decided to go to the same Christian college. College life can be filled with many new exciting good things, but also many dangers. My sister was in a fun-loving group of gals, but that also attracted a fun-loving group of guys. I saw danger signs and became very concerned for my sister's welfare.

We had a Christian Emphasis Week because, even at a Christian college, young men and women need to be challenged in their faith. I was in a dorm prayer group of about six guys when, as we were praying, I was overcome with prayerful concern for my sister. I fell to my knees in tears as I prayed for God to be with her.

I kid you not, while I was still on my knees, the phone at the end of the hall rang (that's how we got phone calls in those days) and a voice yelled out "Murdoch, phone call." I rose from my knees, wiping my tears, as the prayer group was coming to a close, and went to answer the phone. It was my sister's roommate, calling to tell me that my sister had just rededicated her life to the Lord.

+   +   +   +   +   +   +

What can be learned from these four experiences with God during my childhood and teenage years?

1. God was not just there at my drowning experience but God was with me numerous times. Or, was God *always* with me?

2. *All* of these experiences with God happened during difficult times of my life: drowning, sickness, fire, near car crash and a time of crying out to God for my sister. Does God just show up during difficult times in our lives?

   This question reminds me of the analogy of stars in our night sky. The stars are not just up there in the night sky. The stars are also up there in the daytime sky. The difference is that we can only see the stars in times of darkness. Could it be that God is *always* with us but it takes dark times of life for us to see God?

14

God revealed Himself to people and recorded those experiences in the Bible. Let's look at just a few of those experiences.

- *God to Moses during the burning bush:*

  Exodus 3:12 "'I will be with you.'"

- *God to Joshua in his time of fear of becoming a leader:*

  Joshua 1:5 "'I will be with you;'"

- *Jesus to the Disciples as they would start out on their own:*

  Matthew 28:20 "'I am with you always ... '"

We often leave these Scriptures encouraged but still vague about how God is with us. It's similar to receiving a note from a friend that says, "My thoughts are with you." It's a nice note, but what does it mean? How is God present with us and why is it so important to know that God is present with us? Following are some of the Scriptures that answer those questions.

Descriptions of the Tabernacle touch the heart when we understand what is being described.

First, the word "tabernacle" means to dwell with, so God is wanting to live with His people.

15

Exodus 25:8 "'I will dwell among them [you].'"

Second, two key items in the Tabernacle describe God's desire to have His Presence be with His people.

Exodus 25:30 "'bread of the [my] Presence'"— twelve loaves, for all my people. (Also see Leviticus 24:5-9.)

Exodus 25:31 "'lampstand'" – to burn all day and night, as my Presence with you. (Also see Exodus 27:20-21.)

Descriptions of God by David, particularly in the Book of Psalms, further describe the God that David was coming to know as a God whose presence is with us.

Psalm 31:20 "In the shelter of your presence" you keep me safe.

Psalm 41:12 "set me in your presence forever."

Psalm 89:15 "who walk in the light of your presence."

Psalm 139:7 "Where can I flee from your presence?"

The truth of God's presence goes on and on...

- *Through Jesus:*

    Matthew 1:23 "'they will call him Immanuel (which means "God with us").'"

    John 1:14 "The Word became flesh and made his dwelling among us."

- *Through the Holy Spirit:*

    John 14:17 "The Spirit of truth...he lives with you and will be in you."

- *Through eternity:*

    Revelation 21:3 "God's dwelling place is now among the people, and he will dwell with them."

God has always desired to live with us and always will!

Have we not heard?

Have we forgotten?

Have we not understood?

Our God has revealed Himself, not as a God that just shows up at difficult times of life, but as a God who is *always with us*!

(See pages 78-79 for additional personal and/or group study of Chapter Two.)

Chapter Three

GOD REVEALS HIMSELF TO US

God reveals Himself to men and women, boys and girls. We know this is true from so many accounts in the Bible. Let's be reminded of just a few of those accounts.

Genesis 12:1 The LORD said to Abram ...

Genesis 16:7 The angel of the LORD found Hagar ...

Exodus 3:4 God called to Moses from within the bush ...

1 Samuel 3:4 The LORD called to the boy Samuel ...

Matthew 1:20 The angel of the Lord appeared to Joseph in a dream ...

Luke 1:26-27 God sent the angel Gabriel to Mary ...

Acts 12:7 Suddenly an angel of the Lord appeared to Peter ...

In all of these accounts, the message is the same: God reveals Himself to all people—male and female, young and old—and *God knows their situation.*

Some may say God just reveals Himself during the days of the Bible. If that is so, God has changed and no longer reveals Himself. But, if the God of the Bible has not changed, He continues to reveal Himself to male and female, young and old, and *knows your situation!*

When we look at these Old Testament and New Testament accounts, we learn that God is not far away. He is close enough to be involved in our lives. But, there are three questions that deserve our attention.

1. Does God reveal Himself just once to a person or many times?

2. Why does God reveal Himself to us?

3. Does God reveal Himself to all people?

In Chapter One, I wrote about God revealing Himself to me in a drowning experience in a pool at age 10. Is that revelation the end or the beginning of God revealing Himself to me?

In 1971, at age 19, I was part of a college music evangelistic group that traveled to Scandinavia. We were to sing and present Christ in factories, schools, churches, prisons, shopping malls and coffee houses. We were encouraged to keep a diary of our trip and I will include quotes from my diary in this chapter.

We flew from Luxembourg where we would board a train on our way to Scandinavia. One person in our group spoke German and Russian. Otherwise, we were young Americans in a foreign land. We boarded an evening train that would connect and disconnect with other trains along the way through Belgium and Germany.

At one stop, the conductor told us, in German, that we were on the wrong railroad car! We needed to switch to another railroad car, during a five-minute stop, that would be going to our destination which was Copenhagen. It was dark and we needed to quickly gather all our bags, guitars, etc. together to switch into another car.

We barely got switched when we realized that my brown bag with two of our passports was not moved with us into the new railroad car. In broken German and English, we were told that if we got out at the next stop, the car we had first been on would be coming through that stop, now connected to another train on its way to Berlin. If we got off in Cologne, Germany, we would stay in the depot, in the middle of the night, for several hours waiting for the other train to come through. We would then have ten minutes to find the bag!

It was probably 3:00 AM, in a cold January winter. In the night sky, we could see the outline of the Cologne Cathedral, one of the few remnants of the Allied bombing from WWII. We decided to position ourselves along the tracks in the depot, a football field in length, because we did not know where that car would be in the train which was now 20 to 30 cars in length. In the dark, each one of us would jump on trying to find the bag with those passports, running through four or five cars in ten minutes.

After the train stopped, we each hopped on in a different place in this long train. It was hard to see in the dark. All the cars looked the same. The minutes were quickly going by. One of the young women from our group was preparing to jump onto the tracks to stop the train from leaving (crazy Americans)!

The time was running out and I was in the entryway of the last car I was to go through. Out of the corner of my eye, I saw the strip of pale white masking tape that we had put on the end of the dark brown bag to help us identify this bag from many others. It was our bag with the passports! I grabbed the bag and threw it off the train. Then I jumped off, just as the train was leaving!

In my diary entry for January 29, 1971, I wrote, "I was astonished and overflowing. It made my faith grow."

Was this a coincidence? We were young Americans on our way to a mission field. I do not know how God did this, but I believe God revealed His presence with us.

We were in Finland for three months. We traveled with a music group of three Finnish pastors who interpreted for us. One had been a convict earlier in life and then he came to know Jesus and became a pastor. We traveled throughout the country of Finland singing in a variety of venues, but mostly schools around Helsinki, the capital of Finland. We would sing four or five programs each day and then present more of an evangelistic service in the evening at the school.

One night, as we were singing in a packed lunch room, a group of 10 to 12 young men walked into our evangelistic concert. We were told they were a local gang. We had met them earlier at a local youth center.

When we would sing the contemporary American music, they would walk through the crowd to the front row and sit down to enjoy the music. Whenever we would stop the music and give a Christian testimony, they would all stand in unison and walk out through the crowd. When we would begin to sing again, they would walk all the way to the front row and sit down to enjoy the music. When we stopped the music to talk about Jesus, all of them would stand up in unison and walkout.

This continued the whole night! They were making a statement by this disturbance: "We like your music, but we do not want to hear about this Jesus!"

After the service, Finnish teens loved to come up and talk to us, practicing their English and asking for our autographs. This gang also came up to interact with us. Only one of the gang members spoke any English. He was talking with me when the leader of the gang, a kid that looked like he worked out driving trucks without power steering, came up to me and made movements with his arms as he spoke Finnish.

I asked the gang member who spoke English what he was trying to say to me. He said, "He wants to arm wrestle you." Now, we had another college student on our team that looked like he played football. The leader of the gang did not go up to him, but came up to me. I was tall and skinny with toothpicks for arms.

My first response, although not said out loud, was, "You have got to be kidding!" But I knew if I said, "No," he would see Christians talking about Jesus but being afraid. So, I said, "Okay."

We sat down at one of the lunch hall tables, put our elbows on it and prepared to arm wrestle. Then it happened. A voice from within me said, "Just hold your arm firm, don't try to overpower him."

So, I held my arm firm as he continued to try to overpower me and win. I kid you not, this arm wrestling went on for 10 to 15 minutes. I held my arm firm as he kept trying to overpower me. He and other young men who were watching were talking in Finnish.

Then the young man who spoke some English said, "He wonders if you want to call it a draw." I said, "Great!" And the arm wrestling was over, but the conversation was not!

After that, the gang and many others stayed to talk with me. After a while, the custodian said we had to go outside because he needed to lock up the school. With the snow falling, the gang member who spoke English continued to talk with me. The gang even came back the second night.

In my diary entry for March 9, 1971, I wrote, "Talked to them afterwards for an hour. Told them my life story. I pray the Lord works in them."

It happened again: God revealed Himself through an inner voice that gave me direction in what to do and the wisdom and strength to do it!

January through March in Finland is a beautiful winter wonderland, complete with lots of snow, pines and evergreens. Our mission team's homebase was at a camp on one of the many lakes in Finland. We would practice and rejuvenate before heading out to another engagement.

On one of those nights, I needed to be alone for some quiet time. It was probably about 11:00 PM. Under a beautiful starlit sky, I decided to walk out onto the lake covered in ice and snow. I walked on the lake for probably an hour. Then I stopped, knelt and prayed in the middle of the lake, under that beautiful night sky. Just God and me.

When I was ready to return to the lodge, it was too dark to see my tracks. There were numerous lights from cabins scattered along the edge of the lake. Which light was our camp lodge? I started walking in the general direction, heading to a light, only to realize it was not the right light. Eventually, I saw a lodge that looked familiar in the starlit sky and a few lights. It was our camp lodge. I was so thankful to make it safely home to our lodge.

Reflecting back on that night on the ice and snow-covered lake, in the middle of the night, in a foreign land, I wondered how smart it was of me to go out there. I could have fallen through the ice or simply not found my way home. Was God protecting me?

Our time in Finland was coming to a close. There was to be a huge music festival at the University Theatre in Helsinki. There would be our music group, the Finnish pastor's music group and a professional singer from Los Angeles who flew in to join us for this music festival. The theatre held about 1,600 people and it was packed for two days of music and Christian testimonies. Many of the high school students we had met from around Finland were there.

As we finished the last concert, several students came up to greet us and say goodbye. The hall was thinning out. I was walking from the front to the back, with several hundred scattered around in small groups. Then it happened. An inner voice said, "Look to your right."

As I looked, far to the right, against the wall, was a young teenage man that I had met weeks before at one of the schools. He was sitting there alone so I walked across the theatre to the right side and approached him. He saw me and his look said a thousand words. The last time we spoke, several weeks before, we had a very sincere conversation about God and Jesus. He had wanted to become a Christian but his girlfriend didn't want him to take that step. I had this last chance to encourage him in the Christian faith and life.

In my diary entry for April 12, 1971, I wrote, "The one that I prayed to see again, because I felt I should have talked more to him, was there. We went into a small room talked and prayed."

Did God just direct my eyes to see something I would not have seen on my own, just like the beginning of our mission trip when I was in the railroad car?

As I reflect back on that mission trip experience from fifty years ago, it was a time of learning about God. God had revealed himself to me in the swimming pool at age 10, but now, at age 19, God was revealing *more* of Himself to me. So, looking back at the three questions from the beginning of this chapter:

1. <u>Does God reveal Himself once to a person or many times</u>?

   I've always enjoyed the story of Gideon in Judges 6-8. There was nothing special about Gideon. He was a normal guy trying to make a living by farming. There is no reference to Gideon being a friend of God or of service to God, until God sends His angel to Gideon. This is the beginning of many times and ways God reveals Himself to Gideon.

   Judges 6:12 God's angel speaks to Gideon ...

   Judges 6:23 God directly speaks words of encouragement to Gideon ...

   Judges 6:34 The Spirit of the LORD comes upon Gideon ...

   Judges 7:2 The LORD speaks directly to Gideon ...

Judges 7:10 God is patient with Gideon ...

So, God does not speak just once to Gideon, but many times through his life and in different ways. And I believe that God reveals Himself and speaks to *us* many times and in different ways.

In my diary entry for February 11, 1971, I wrote, "The Holy Spirit will work through anyone who will give themselves completely to Christ. Trust and obey!"

2. Why does God reveal Himself to us?

I have always enjoyed the story of Joseph in Genesis 37-50. Here we have one of the youngest sons of Jacob so we might expect him to do great things. He comes from an important, yet dysfunctional, family. But, we find that he is a spoiled young man with a very prideful attitude. Now, he is sold as a slave so that seems to be the end of this important young man. But, at the end of the story, Joseph analytically and prophetically says to his brothers, as recorded in Genesis 50:20, that God used *all* the troubles he had in his life for "'the saving of many lives [people].'"

God always reveals Himself for a purpose, His purpose, which always centers itself around the saving of many people.

So, if God reveals Himself to you, *stay humble.* It's not about you and whether you are better or more important than others. It's about God's plan to use you, in His plan, for the saving of many people!

3. <u>Does God reveal Himself to all people?</u>

I have grown to appreciate the story of the woman at the well in John 4. We don't have her name. Perhaps this story is about many nameless people. Perhaps this story is about all the people who feel rejected and burdened by their mistakes in life. We know that she is just going about her daily life of getting water. Sounds pretty uneventful, until Jesus shows up and begins a conversation with her. Her first comment to him is something like, "Why are you talking to me? I'm not important!" We know from the Scripture that she has been married and divorced five times. Every husband threw her away so now she has a man that will just use her.

As the conversation goes on, Jesus says, "I am the Messiah" (the *One* who comes to make things *right*). Jesus can reveal himself to all people, even to a broken and desperate woman.

We must be very careful about saying God will reveal himself to the worthy but won't reveal himself to the broken and desperate. God reveals Himself to more people than we can possibly imagine!

God's purpose for revealing Himself is consistent. It's about the saving of many people. The woman at the well went into town and told others about Jesus and many believed in Him!

(See pages 80-81 for additional personal and/or group study of Chapter Three.)

Chapter Four

IMPORTANT POINTS TO REVIEW – I

Reviewing the following chapters:

1. SEEING GOD'S HAND

2. LEARNING TO WATCH FOR GOD

3. GOD REVEALS HIMSELF

It is good to review several important key points from these chapters.

1. <u>God uses the hard times in our life for good.</u>

   These stories included sickness, tragedies and troubles. We often grieve over the troubles of our life. Yet, these were the times God brought about the greatest good! Perhaps we need to change our vision from seeing the tragedy to looking for the good God will bring through the tragedy!

2. <u>It usually takes the dark times of life for us to see God.</u>

   Think about the many Bible characters and their experiences with the dark times of life. It is a repeated theme in the Old and New Testaments.

   Remember Moses and the people of God at the Red Sea, with Pharoah's chariots charging from behind, and the sea blocking their way forward? It was an incredibly dark moment. Yet, that's when they saw God.

Remember Peter in prison? James had just been beheaded. Peter had little hope of release. It was an incredibly dark moment. Yet, that's when he heard God.

Perhaps it's the same with God and us. It's in the incredibly dark moments of life that we can most easily see God.

3. God is *always* with us.

This concept can *transform* how we go through life. Check out your prayers. Do you pray that God will show up and help you in a difficult time, **or** do you pray knowing that God is already with you? It's like the difference of communicating with someone who lives far away versus communicating with someone sitting next to you. What if we lived our lives praying and knowing that God is already with us?

4. God speaks to us many times throughout our lives.

So, learn to listen for His voice and watch for His hand, His fingerprints.

There was a Christian woman who called me to see if she could stop by my office. She was leaving her doctor's office where she was just diagnosed with terminal cancer. As she told me her diagnosis and shed some tears, I told her we would pray for her healing and God's presence to be with her in this journey. I then said, "Watch for God's fingerprints along the way."

Several months later, on the day before her death, she said to me, "Do you remember when you told me to watch for God's fingerprints?" I responded, "Yes." She said, "I saw God's fingerprints." I responded, "I know, because God is always faithful!"

5. <u>God reveals Himself to us for the saving of many people.</u>

Early in my ministry, there was a woman who started coming to church who had five children by five different men. As I talked with her about life and faith, she told me that she was afraid to die. I told her why Jesus came and she decided to accept Jesus into her life.

Sometime later, she was taken to Intensive Care at the local hospital. When I walked into her Intensive Care ward, the nurse told me that they had a code blue on her that night.

When I walked toward her bed, she started yelling to me, repeatedly saying, "I'm not afraid to die anymore. I'm not afraid to die anymore." She then told me that she had met Jesus, "and he has a beard, just like they say!" She added, "I am no longer afraid to die."

33

Several months later, at her funeral, I shared how she had met Jesus and was no longer afraid to die.

6. <u>God reveals Himself during the ordinary activities of life.</u>

God reveals Himself in times of worship and prayer, but the Scriptures and my experiences tell me that He reveals Himself most often in the ordinary activities of life—things like swimming lessons, driving the car, on a trip and during illness.

So, let's open our eyes and watch for God, because He is *already* there!

(See pages 82-83 for additional personal and/or group study of Chapter Four.)

Chapter Five

WHY ARE WE AFRAID?

Looking back at the many stories of God revealing Himself to me, you may think that I never struggled with worry and discouragement. Yet, I must admit that even after all the times God revealed Himself to me, I continued to struggle with <u>fear</u>, <u>doubt</u>, <u>worry</u> and <u>discouragement</u>. Why?

Why do we still walk in the shadows of a life of <u>fear</u>, <u>doubt</u>, <u>worry</u> and <u>discouragement</u>?

Let's look at three accounts of Scriptures from the Old Testament, New Testament and the Letters of Paul. These Scriptures cover nearly 2,000 years of God and His people.

<u>God and Moses: Exodus 3-4</u>

This is a powerful account of God speaking to Moses in a burning bush. God says that He sees His people suffering under Pharoah and that He is going to rescue them by sending Moses. Imagine, Moses is having one of the greatest experiences with God, and yet, Moses still <u>doubts</u>. As the account continues, God turns Moses' staff into a snake. Moses runs from the snake, but he also runs from God's plan to save many people. Why? He's <u>afraid</u>.

Why in the midst of God revealing Himself to Moses is Moses still controlled by <u>doubt</u> and <u>fear</u>?

Jesus and the Disciples: Matthew 14

This is a powerful account of Jesus feeding 5,000 men plus the women and children with five loaves of bread and two small fish. After this miracle, you would think the disciples would be riding the "high" of faith, but the following verse says, *immediately* Jesus sent the disciples in a boat onto the Sea of Galilee.

It was now the middle of the night with the wind and waves knocking them around, and then they think a ghost appears on the water next to them. Talk about a rough night!

Jesus calls out to them, "'Take courage. It is I. Don't be afraid'" (Matt. 14:27). Peter got out of the boat. Peter was the only one of the twelve with courage to do so. You have to admire Peter's faith, but then he sees the wind and waves and he is <u>afraid</u> and begins to sink. Jesus reaches out and saves Peter, but then Jesus says, "'why did you doubt?'" (Matt. 14:31).

Why in the midst of a miraculous day of feeding more than 5,000 people and seeing Jesus miraculously walking on the water are the disciples still <u>afraid</u>?

Paul's Last Letter to Timothy: 2 Timothy 1-4

Timothy sincerely committed his life to Jesus at a young age. He was mentored by Paul, the greatest teacher of the early church. He received the gift of the Holy Spirit to help him in his life and his ministry. He was now the leader of the church of Ephesus. Yet, Paul makes the following comments to Timothy:

- "I constantly remember you in my prayers" (2 Tim. 1:3).
  Did Timothy need to know he was prayed for?

- "fan into flame the gift of God, which is in you" (2 Tim. 1:6).
  Was the flame going out?

- "Guard the good deposit entrusted to you" (2 Tim. 1:14).
  Was it in danger of being lost?

- "be strong" (2 Tim. 2:1).
  Was he weak?

- "continue in what you have learned" (2 Tim. 3:14).
  Was he in danger of quitting?

- "keep your head in all situations" (2 Tim. 4:5).
  Was he struggling to keep it together?

Doesn't this sound like a coach trying to encourage a player at halftime as he is losing the game? Is Timothy struggling with <u>fear</u>, <u>doubt</u>, <u>worry</u> and <u>discouragement</u>? If so, why?

Are we doomed, as people of faith, to still walk in the shadow of <u>fear</u>, <u>doubt</u>, <u>worry</u> and <u>discouragement</u>? What can we learn from these Scriptures?

1. God never gave up on Moses, Jesus never gave up on the disciples and Paul never gave up on Timothy. In fact, these men who were afraid and doubted were used by God to change the world. Just because you struggle with <u>fear</u>, <u>doubt</u>, <u>worry</u> and <u>discouragement</u> does not mean God will give up on you. In fact, what the Scriptures teach us is just the opposite: You may doubt, but God will be faithful to you!

2. As Moses continued to walk with God, he learned to walk in faith, even more. As the disciples continued to walk with Jesus, the disciples grew in their faith, especially after Jesus had risen and they received the Holy Spirit. As Timothy continued to run his race, there came a day when he, like Paul, said, "I have fought the good fight, I have finished the race, I have kept the faith" (2 Tim. 4:7).

3. One of my greatest joys of ministry was time spent with older Christians. I would hear their accounts of struggle and tragedy but I still saw in them a perseverance that shone like a mighty beacon. Don't get me wrong, they weren't perfect; but they had survived the storms and still their light was shining bright. How did they do it? And, how can we do it?

There's a very clear answer and a Scripture verse that speaks to how to not let the <u>fears</u> and <u>doubts</u> overwhelm you. It was the early days of the church. There were dangers, fears and opposition. Yet, they learned a way to make it through. "They devoted themselves to the apostles' teaching and to fellowship, to the breaking of bread and to prayer" (Acts 2:42).

One of the greatest tragedies I have seen as a pastor is, after a Christian goes through a tragedy of life (illness, death of a loved one, bankruptcy, etc.), they separate themselves from other believers. Perhaps they feel that God failed them, the church failed them or that they failed God. Like the analogy of separating a burning coal from a fire, away from the fire, it will soon go out. After going through tragedies, what is needed is getting even closer to the fire.

If we are to see victory over <u>fear</u>, <u>doubt</u>, <u>worry</u> and <u>discouragement</u>, we must devote ourselves:

- To the teaching

- To the fellowship

- To the breaking of bread

- To prayer

- ***The rest is left to God!!!***

There is a story of a Christian man going through a great struggle in his family. As he was going through this great struggle, he was not able to have a good night's rest and he was not able to eat well. He was losing weight and losing the battle with <u>fear</u>, <u>doubt</u>, <u>worry</u> and <u>discouragement</u>.

In one of those sleepless nights, he cried out to God, "Why is this happening?" and there was a voice. It was as clear as a bell. The voice said, "*Trust*." He looked over to his wife thinking she had spoken, but she was asleep. Who spoke? The voice was so clear and strong. Just one word, "*Trust!!!*" From that one word, he could go forward knowing God was there, even during that great struggle.

The struggle with walking in the shadow of <u>fear</u>, <u>doubt</u>, <u>worry</u> and <u>discouragement</u> is common to all. Yet, we can learn to walk in the light of knowing that God goes before us.

(See pages 84-85 for additional personal and/or group study of Chapter Five.)

Chapter Six

WHAT DO YOU SEE?

(**Note:** Names or details may have been altered to maintain confidentiality.)

What do you see when you meet someone? Do you look at what they are wearing or do you see their age, weight or height? Do you see a saint or sinner or assess their condition in life?

As you ponder these questions, it's important to ask, "What did Jesus see when he met people?" What did Jesus see when he met the woman at the well or Mary Magdalene? What did Jesus see when he met Zacchaeus or Peter?

It's then equally important to ask the question: How do you see yourself? Do you see yourself as strong or weak? Do you see yourself as a failure or successful? Do you see yourself as a saint or sinner? Do you see yourself as never good enough or ugly?

As you ponder these questions, it's important to ask, "What does Jesus see when he sees you?" Does Jesus see your successes or failures? Does Jesus see your sin or weakness?

How we see others *and* ourselves is so important! We either see others and ourselves through a worldly view or we see others *and* ourselves through "a Jesus view."

Jesus' view of people (others and ourselves) is built upon the foundation of how God sees people, *all people*.

"So God created mankind in his own image, in the image of God he created them; male and female he created them" (Genesis 1:27).

Being involved in our church's jail ministry helped to "open my eyes." These men and women, of all ages, had one thing in common. They all wore "orange suits." But I learned to say to them, "You were not created to wear an orange suit." Every one of these inmates was born in the image of their Heavenly Father. So, what happened?

As I got to know these inmates, I would often attend their court hearings as they appeared before a judge. In a courtroom, I noticed several important things.

1. There were usually many others wearing "orange suits."

2. Many of these inmates had family or loved ones who were there to support them. When they saw the inmate, they saw them as their child, grandchild or loved one and not as someone in an "orange suit."

3. A judgement would be placed upon the inmate: You are a thief, a repeat offender, a danger to society, etc. But is that who they were?

4. I would then see their picture in the newspaper declaring the conviction of the person in the "orange suit"—this child, grandchild or loved one. So now the community saw them as someone in an "orange suit" and *not* as a child, grandchild or loved one.

5. I also wondered how they saw themselves. Did they see themselves as someone in an "orange suit" or as someone who is loved?

"So God created mankind in his own image, in the image of God he created them; male and female he created them" (Genesis 1:27).

This verse is such a powerful verse that can transform our view of *every* human being!!! This verse can transform how we see everyone, regardless of race, gender, creed or the "suit" they wear. This verse can also transform how we see ourselves, regardless of our income or stature. Tragically, so many people see themselves as less than who they really are. These negative self-views are **so** destructive!

+   +   +   +   +   +   +

What did Jesus see when he saw the "woman at the well" in John 4:7? She was a Samaritan so she dressed a little different. She was getting water at noon, an unusual time. Most would get their water in the cool of the day. Jesus saw these things but he especially noted that she had been married and divorced five times and was now shacking up with another man.

Tara came to church with her children. Her face was worn but she seemed to smile through the scars of her life. In her youth, she had been sexually abused by a leader at the YMCA. As she carried this hidden secret, she chose to live a lesbian lifestyle, only to continue to feel empty and betrayed. She later married a man and gave birth to their children, but the hidden shame was still there.

As she shook hands at the door following the church service, you could see her desire for a safe and good place for her children. You could also see the hidden pain in her eyes from the secret she still carried.

The day of her baptism was a glorious day that led to years of fulfillment, acceptance and involvement in the church family, the Body of Christ. Her smile became even greater as you could now see that she no longer carried the secret and shame.

In John 4, after meeting Jesus, the "woman at the well" goes into town, to the people she had been ashamed to see in the cool of the day, and tells them to come meet a man who "told me everything I ever did. Could he be the Messiah?" Could he be the Christ, the one who came to make everything right?

+   +   +   +   +   +   +

What did Jesus see when he saw Mary Magdalene in Luke 8:2? Did he see the local crazy woman? What does someone with seven demons in them act like?

Katie saw her life as the product of a very difficult childhood. There had been physical abuse that left scars that continued to affect her life and relationships. Trying to numb the pain of her childhood, she turned to drugs and alcohol, only to wake up to her continued torment. As she entered relationships and marriage, they always ended up in brokenness. Then came the death of her parents and she felt so alone.

One Sunday as she was sitting in her car in the parking lot of a shopping mall, she heard a local church service radio broadcast. The message that Sunday was about Jesus who can bring the power of forgiveness and hope of a new life.

She entered that church's doors the next Sunday and never left the Christian community. She experienced the power to forgive those who hurt her and the power to forgive herself. She experienced the reality of a better life, a life she never thought was possible.

After Mary Magdalene met Jesus, she never left the Christian community. Mary was next to Jesus at the cross. Mary was there at the empty tomb. Mary was the first person to announce, "*Jesus is risen!!!*"

+   +   +   +   +   +   +

What did Jesus see when he saw Zacchaeus in Luke 19:1-4? He was a "chief tax collector" and was wealthy. The point being, he didn't get his wealth through honest work. He sold out his neighbors and charged them extra taxes when he wanted to pad his pockets. He was also a "short" and "despised man."

Reagan was a businessman. He had grown up going to a church but he felt that God had long ago forgotten about him. His life had been filled with the goal of making as much money as possible and having a "good time" in the process. His ex-wives saw him as a self-centered man and his children were very distant.

Why he came to church that first Sunday can only be described as he was looking for something to fill his emptiness. Shaking his hand at the door, I asked if he'd ever want to get together and visit. Before he realized it, he had said yes and the meeting was set.

That first meeting included a perplexing question for me: "Why would you, as a pastor, want to spend time with me? If you knew all that I have done, you wouldn't want to spend time with me!" My response was, "Every man is God's son and is important to God. And, whatever you have done, Jesus has come to forgive you and give you a new life." There was discussion on whether this could really be true. Upon realizing that God could accept him and forgive him, he was ready to commit fully to this new life.

Jesus invited himself to Zacchaeus's house. There and then, that day, Zacchaeus gave up his old life and began to live a new life.

+   +   +   +   +   +   +

What did Jesus see when he saw Peter in Matthew 4:18? He was a fisherman. What have you smelled like after a full day of fishing? Fishing was not a clean occupation so it was hard to be clean enough for a traditional religious lifestyle.

David had a little faith background but his life had been consumed by doing what he needed to do to pay the bills. This led to a lifestyle of living *in* the world and *like* the world.

He had a college education so he was no dummy, but his work and broken marriages led him to a life of drinking in order to numb the pain. It was like nothing could be done to change his life.

Why he came to church that first Sunday, I do not remember, but I know it was a time of desperation and contemplating suicide. As I shook his hand following the worship service, I asked if he wanted to get together and visit. He quickly said, "Yes," and our appointment was set.

He talked about his brokenness and emptiness in life. I grieved with him, but stated that God had more for him in life than what he knew. He was intrigued by the idea that the God of the universe could have something more for him in life.

We started meeting regularly and reading Scriptures. He absorbed the Scriptures as if he was starving for this newfound food. He desired more from the "banquet table." He was baptized and joined small groups. Then the day came when he began to lead and teach these small groups.

In time, Jesus changed Simon's name, the name of the fisherman, to Peter, which means "the rock." Jesus then declared the church would be built upon Peter, the rock.

+   +   +   +   +   +   +

What can we learn from these stories?

1. Look at the self-view of each character in the Bible:

   - The woman at the well – After five divorces, she wondered if there was hope for her.

   - Mary Magdalene – Seven demons seemed overwhelming.

   - Zacchaeus – He had money but was looking for something greater.

   - Peter – He thought he could never be clean enough.

2. Look at the self-view of each contemporary character:

   - Tara – After carrying her hidden secret, she wondered if there was hope for her.

   - Katie – Was forgiveness even possible for her?

- Reagan – Could there be new life for him?

- David – He was so hungry for something new.

What did Jesus see in each one that they could not see in themselves?

1. Jesus saw them from God's perspective—that each one was created in the image of God; that there is nothing cheap or hopeless about someone created in the image of God!

2. Jesus saw *not* their past but their potential—that even though each one had scars, they were created to be useful in God's Kingdom's work. Each one of these Gospel and contemporary characters went on to be used as a "difference maker" in God's Kingdom's work. ***Amazing!***

Can we see people like Jesus sees people?

1. This is really a *very* significant question! Because if we can't, then how are men and women to become "difference makers" in the Kingdom of God?

2. Look beyond the "orange suit" or whatever they may be wearing *and look into their eyes!*

+   +   +   +   +   +   +

Lanny was unknown to me but was well known by God. He had grown up in a Christian church-going family.

There were hurts as a boy that no one knew except God and the perpetrator. Like many other boys that grew up going to church, he also stopped going to church as a teenager. Life then became centered around sports and girls.

Life always goes by so fast. He was now a father of teenagers. Then came an invitation to a free barbeque in the park. Some other men he knew and I were putting on this free "gourmet" barbeque in the park. So, he came for the food but experienced something so much more! I was greeting everyone and when I came to Lanny, I said, "I see God in your eyes!" How could God be seen in his eyes?

> "So God created mankind in his own image, in the image of God he created them; male and female he created them" (Genesis 1:27).

I could see the Heavenly Father in the man's eyes. *Wow!* The hurts from boyhood, the wrong choices as a teenager and the godless life as a man could still not take away the fact that "he was still his Father's son!"

In the weeks that followed, Lanny entered a church for the first time in many years. He and I talked through the hurts and sins of his life. And then we looked at the Scriptures that teach about the God of the Bible. This God is the God for young boys but also the God for men. Today, Lanny continues to be a reflection of his Heavenly Father wherever he goes!

+   +   +   +   +   +   +

Roy was in familiar surroundings—the County Jail. But something changed this time that would affect the rest of his life. He asked to see a pastor and I was contacted. As I entered the enclosed room, Roy was on one side of the glass and I was on the opposite side of the glass. We could see each other but had to talk using phones.

After the opening comments of, "Who are you?" and "How can I be helpful?", it was as if the floodgates had opened and out came all the regrets and confessions of a young man's life, one who had even missed all of his children's birthdays. There were questions: "Is there any hope for me?" "Can I ever be forgiven?" "Can anyone love me?"

You only continue to visit an inmate if requested by them and, even then, only so often. But this first encounter led to weekly visits over the next year. As the weeks went by, Roy received his own Bible and began to immerse himself into God's Word. Within six months, he had read the whole Bible.

Then came the day he was released from jail. He was sitting in church the first Sunday he was out of jail. Every week he met with me as he continued "to dine on the *Bread of Life*." He was baptized and started to attend small groups in the church. Then the day came that he shared his testimony and we rejoiced in God's goodness. Then he began to lead small groups and even preach some sermons. Today, Roy continues to be a light for God where ever he goes!

+   +   +   +   +   +   +

Kyle was unknown to me (but well known by God) until the tragic day of his brother's death. It is always so difficult to hear of the death of a teenager; but as word rippled through the community, it eventually affected everyone's home.

My heart was touched by this tragedy so I sent a note of encouragement to Kyle. I did not know Kyle but my daughter was in school with him. In one note, I opened the door to meet to visit about his brother's death, if he wanted to. Kyle did not know me but accepted the invitation.

The first meeting centered on the death of his brother and eternal questions of heaven and hell. Then the discussion turned to Kyle's own life and faith. Kyle had serious questions but he was also a serious student. He wanted to learn what the Bible had to say.

He started to meet weekly with me, studying Scriptures and seeing how they related to his own life's choices and decisions. He asked Jesus into his heart, to forgive his sins and be his Lord. He was baptized. He helped start a men's group where honest questions from and for men were discussed. Through studies and other discussions, he became enthralled by the life of Billy Graham—how Billy Graham came to the Lord and then became an evangelist.

Kyle then felt called into God's work, specifically speaking to teenagers. He felt God wanted him to help teens with their choices of life and faith. The Holy Spirit touched his heart with the verse from the Sermon on the Mount (Matthew 7:13): "'Enter through the narrow gate. For wide is the gate and broad is the road that leads to destruction, and many enter through it.'"

Today, Kyle continues in the calling God has placed on his heart!

+   +   +   +   +   +   +

NOT ALL STORIES HAVE A HAPPY ENDING

- *1 Samuel 15:11* "'I regret that I have made Saul king,'"

  God Almighty grieved over the fact that he made Saul a king.

- *Matthew 19:21-22* "'Then come, follow me.' When the young man heard this, he went away sad,"

  Jesus was calling a young man who would not give up his old ways.

- *2 Timothy 4:10* "for Demas, because he loved this world, has deserted me"

  Paul had discipled Demas who later turned away.

+   +   +   +   +   +   +

Lois grew up in a devoted Christian family. She dearly loved the Lord. As life went on, she married, raised several children and continued to live out her Christian faith—until one of the most hurtful things of marriage happened. Her husband committed adultery. The family kind of survived but Lois's core was changed forever. She became a bitter, bitter woman. She was a woman scorned!

Tragically, it was as if her Christian spirit was uprooted. She could not forgive and would not forgive. This decision led to other tragic influences upon her children and grandchildren for the rest of her life.

+   +   +   +   +   +   +

Mark and Penny were a delightful couple but had a lot of chaos in their relationship. Their kids were growing up quickly. The things that caused chaos in their marriage soon became amplified as the choices of their teenagers only multiplied the chaos in their home.

I saw all the possibilities in the world for this young family and tried to love them and teach them about forgiveness and grace offered through Jesus. I tried to guide them out of the chaos in which they were living. But, in time, they chose the life of chaos over anything I, as their pastor, or Jesus had to offer!

+   +   +   +   +   +   +

Stuart and Janet entered the church doors with their children, displaying a strong love for the Lord. They had experienced a lot of church life and expressed the betrayal of many Christian friends. They were a very talented couple and were willing to help out with ministries in the church.

But, the love of the world is a strong magnet. There is the desire for the finer things of life, the things money can buy. Then there are the desired friendships with the rich and the "pretty people" of this world. All these things create an aura of self-attainment and self-righteousness. Then to find out that they were actually working against God's Kingdom!

+ + + + + + +

Some would say that you are wasting your time by reaching out to people who might turn away. But, if some turned away from God, Jesus and Paul, should we not expect that some will turn away from us? This does not mean failure!

So, *open your eyes* and *look into the eyes* of every man, woman and child you meet and see them as created in the image of God—created to be a part of God's Kingdom's work.

(See pages 86-87 for additional personal and/or group study of Chapter Six.)

Chapter Seven

ON DEATH BEDS

What's happening when people are in the process of dying? Early in my ministry, God taught me about the importance of the time of someone's death!

+   +   +   +   +   +   +

Floyd had been a member of the church for a long, long time. I came to know him and his wife, Alta, as an older couple in the church. He was a former mayor of the community. He was a Sunday School teacher, a Trustee and a respected leader of the church and community.

Alta came down with Alzheimer's and was admitted into a care home. Floyd continued to live on his own and faithfully visited her. They had no children or grandchildren, only distant relatives.

Eventually, Floyd entered the hospital with heart failure and died within days of his admittance. On one of my visits to see him in the hospital, he asked me, "Will God ever forgive me?"

I was a very young pastor and still in seminary. I was taken aback by his question and wondered what he had done that, on his death bed and as a leader in the church, caused him to wonder whether he could be forgiven.

I responded, "Jesus came to forgive us," thinking maybe he had committed some moral sin. Floyd then continued, "I did not do with my money what I should have done!"

How sad that, at the end of his life, he was afraid that his sin of omission, of not doing what he should have done with his money, was weighing on his heart.

+   +   +   +   +   +   +

Captain Porter was a tall and dapper older gentleman. He was strikingly handsome in his beige suit and Stetson hat, using a cane and usually chewing on a cigar. Captain Porter got his name from being a Captain in WWI in the trenches of France. He had been exposed to mustard gas in that war.

As it comes to every man to die, he had entered the hospital and was now in the last days of his life. On one of my visits with him, he told me the following story.

A role of the Captain in WWI was to speak, while standing on a platform, to the troops before they would go into battle. His talk would be followed by a chaplain who would say a prayer for the troops. Captain Porter had a young assistant who said he was an atheist. So, the young assistant dismissed the importance of prayer before battle!

One morning, after Captain Porter spoke to the troops and the chaplain said the prayer, Captain Porter stepped off the platform and went around and behind the platform where, to his surprise, he saw the young assistant kneeling in the mud. Captain Porter reached down to him and asked if he was okay. The young assistant responded with a stark look in his eyes, and said, "Today, I die!" Captain Porter, lying on *his* death bed, told me this story and concluded, "And he died that day!"

+   +   +   +   +   +   +

Visiting Pearl in the care home was always a special time. She was a typical Christian widow who was now finishing her life in a 15- x 20-foot room. Yet, she was very content.

On one of those visits, Pearl told me she had a story to tell me. She began, "Did you know that I had a son die in France in WWII?" I responded, "No, I did not know that part of your life." Then she told me the following story.

"In the middle of the night, when my son was fighting in WWII, I was awakened with the sound of his voice calling out to me, 'Mom, Mom!'" She said, "I knew he had just died!" Several weeks later, she received word from the government that her son indeed had died that night!

+   +   +   +   +   +   +

Have you ever been with someone in the days before their death? If they are unconscious, we typically are quiet, not wanting to disturb them. The following two accounts are of men, on their death beds, who had not responded for days.

+   +   +   +   +   +   +

Arlie was alone and lying on his hospital bed as I walked in to check on him. He had been in the hospital for several weeks and his condition was declining. He was now unresponsive.

So, as I sat next to his bed with no one to talk with, I began to read some Scriptures out loud. I had read Psalm 23 and a few verses of Philippians 4. When I came to Philippians 4:13 and began reading, "I can do...", Arlie joined me in quoting the rest of the verse, "... all this [everything] through him who gives me strength."

I looked at him, amazed at what had just happened! As far as I know, he never spoke another word before his death the next day.

+   +   +   +   +   +   +

Everett was usually in the worship service with his wife. They would sit in the back row, as far from the front as possible. His wife, Dorothy, was always very engaged in worship, singing from her soul and smiling through the whole sermon. Everett, on the other hand, would stand for a hymn but never sing.

Everett's health declined and he was now on his death bed in this small government-subsidized apartment. Shortly before his death, I stopped by for one of my visits. He had not responded for several days. A nurse and about a dozen family and friends were crowded together and visiting around his bed. Everett lay motionless on his bed. I asked his wife, Dorothy, if we could sing a few songs and she enthusiastically agreed.

We sang a couple of familiar songs, "How Great Thou Art" and "Amazing Grace," when, to our surprise, Everett lifted his left arm and started to direct us, on beat, like a choir director. At the end of the song, he lowered his arm and never moved again before his death the next day!

+   +   +   +   +   +   +

The story of Linda is one of the accounts I referred to earlier in my writing. Linda was a wonderful Christian woman. She and her husband had served in ministry to students. They had also raised a house full of children and enjoyed family and faith.

One day as I was in my office, Linda called. She was just leaving her doctor's office and asked if she could stop by to see me. So, about 15 minutes later, we sat together in my office. She had just been told that she had a very aggressive terminal cancer and had only months to live. She was strong and said she was not afraid to die but she would miss leaving her family. My role was to listen, encourage and try to be a voice for God. We prayed for God to heal her, which is always right. And then I said, "Watch for God's fingerprints."

The months went by and she was now on her death bed. As I visited with her and her husband, she wanted to talk to me alone. As I sat close to her death bed so I could hear her weak voice, she said, "Do you remember when you told me to watch for God's fingerprints?" I responded that I did. She then continued, "I saw God's fingerprints!"

+   +   +   +   +   +   +

Pauline was a vivacious older woman. She was as wide as she was tall and her laughter filled the room. She started coming to church with her daughter's family after she moved into town. The daughter told me that Pauline was not a church goer. Before coming to this town, she had lived in a small nearby town and had five children by five different men.

I had asked Pauline if she would like to visit sometime. She said she would. When we started to visit, she quickly shared that she was afraid to die. That comment is not unusual, but she was a bold woman, cutting right to the quick. We talked about Jesus and that he had come to forgive our sins and give us eternal life.

The months went by and I received an early morning phone call from the hospital. Pauline had been brought into ICU with a "code blue." I walked into the Intensive Care Unit, with only curtains between each patient. Pauline was in the far-left bed. She saw me coming and started yelling my name. You are supposed to be quiet in ICU, so I hurried to Pauline's bedside.

The first thing she said to me was, "I'm not afraid to die anymore!" I asked, "Pauline, what happened?" She responded, "You know how I've always been afraid to die?" I said, "Yes." She again repeated, "I'm not afraid to die anymore! This went on two or more times and I finally said firmly, "Pauline, what happened?" She then told me the following story. (*Notice the details.*)

"Last night I died. I was up in the corner of the ceiling, looking down at my body and they were pounding on my chest, but it didn't hurt. The next thing I knew, I was going through clouds toward a very bright light. When I arrived at the light, it was the most beautiful place with trees, flowers and green grass. Then I saw my family and they all came over to greet me.

"Then I saw Jesus and he has a beard just like they say! Then Jesus came to me and said I needed to go back, but I told him, '*No*, I won't go back.' But Jesus told me I had to go back, but that before long, he would come for me. The next thing I knew, I was waking up. And, I'm not afraid to die anymore!"

Two months later she died and I shared this story at her funeral.

+　　　+　　　+　　　+　　　+　　　+　　　+

Randy was one of the most interesting guys that I had ever met in my early ministry. He was just a little older than me. The first time I met him was in the county jail when I was visiting one of the teenagers from our church. Randy asked who I was and why I was at the jail. Then he asked if I would also visit him. That began my relationship and story with Randy.

Months went by and he was out of jail. He started coming to church. He asked Jesus into his heart.

One time while visiting Randy, I met his parents. They were hardened people and suspicious of me as a preacher. Then the day came when Randy wasn't in church and he didn't respond to many of my phone calls. He said he had a new job, was making good money, had a new girlfriend, but that he would be back.

Late one afternoon as I was walking our little dog out by the street, guess who drove by? Randy. He was driving a new car and he stopped to say, "Hi." I knelt next to the car so we could talk since he was in the driver's seat behind the steering wheel. We chatted and I told him that I had missed him in church. He responded, "I learned something. You only need God when you're in trouble." I was speechless. I did not know what to say! We ended the conversation and he drove off.

Sometime later, there was Randy, sitting in the back row of church, on a Sunday morning. He was nearly the last one to leave the service and we greeted each other at the door. He asked if I could meet that afternoon. So, at 3 PM that Sunday afternoon, I met with Randy in my office.

The discussion quickly became very somber. He asked, "Will God ever forgive me?" He then told me that he had gotten into trouble dealing with drugs and all that goes with it. He was crying. I said Jesus came to forgive us and there's nothing that he can do that Jesus can't forgive. There was more sharing, a time of confession and prayer. When he left the office, he was almost skipping, now assured of the forgiveness of Jesus.

Later that night, about 3 AM, the phone rang. I answered and on the phone was Randy's mother. She said, "Randy is dead!" She went on to say that someone had killed him. It was the only time I have seen a body on a marble slab with three bullet holes in the chest.

+   +   +   +   +   +   +

NOTE: All of these stories have a lot of differences, but they also have one thing in common. They all speak of God's presence, in some way, at death!

Psalm 23:4
Even though I walk through the darkest valley
[the valley of the shadow of death] ...
you are with me.

(See pages 88-89 for additional personal and/or group study of Chapter Seven.)

Chapter Eight

IMPORTANT POINTS TO REVIEW – II

Reviewing the following chapters:

1. WHY ARE WE AFRAID?

2. WHAT DO YOU SEE?

3. ON DEATH BEDS

You will find these three chapters contain key points that relate to every human being, including you. Also, you will find all three chapters speak to one key point about the heart of God—*God's eternal love for mankind!* When we are tempted to give up on ourselves or others, God's eternal love continues to pursue us even to our death beds!

+   +   +   +   +   +   +

Discussion about the Bible story of Jonah usually centers around the whale and, in so doing, misses the *larger* points of the story. God wanted the prophet Jonah to go to the great and wicked city of Nineveh to tell them to repent or else God would destroy them. Jonah did not want to do this *because,* as recorded in Jonah 4:2, "'I knew that you are a gracious and compassionate God, slow to anger and abounding in love, a God who relents from sending calamity.'" Jonah knew that God loved the wicked people of Nineveh, enemies of Israel, and Jonah could not accept this!

+   +   +   +   +   +   +

Doing a chapel service in a jail is a wonderful experience. One time while doing a chapel service, the room was completely full of inmates. The topic was the God of the Bible who could forgive sins through Jesus. All the inmates were comforted to hear these words until I said, "God can forgive anyone for any sin."

A young man in the back row of the room raised his hand and said, "God cannot forgive a child molester."

Everyone found comfort in the belief that, through Jesus, *they* could be forgiven for their sins but *not that others* could be forgiven for their sins.

Does this jail dining room chapel mirror most Christian congregations and most Christians? Do we too often put a limit on God's love and forgiveness, just like Jonah and just like the inmate in the jail?

+   +   +   +   +   +   +

Jack was a young man that attended church with his wife and children. Eventually, he sought some time with me for some personal conversation. He wanted to ask if he could be forgiven for something he had done as a teenager. He had molested his little sister. What would you say to him?

Phil was a young man who came to church with his family. He was a delightful young man. One day, as we shared pizza, he stated that he had done something as a youth for which he could never be forgiven. He had molested a younger male cousin. What would you say to him?

Do you place limits on God's love and forgiveness? Jack asked if he could be forgiven and has grown into a wonderful Christian man. Phil said he could never be forgiven and, no matter what the professional counselor, I or the Scriptures said, he continued to say it was impossible for him to be forgiven. He eventually committed suicide. "'Those who cling to worthless idols turn away from God's love for them'" (Jonah 2:8).

+   +   +   +   +   +   +

God said in the Ten Commandments: "'You shall not murder'" (Exodus 20:13). Yet, have you considered that both Moses and Paul (named Saul at the time) were murderers (Exodus 2:12 and Acts 8:1)? Why does God do this to our comfortable view of life and faith?

+   +   +   +   +   +   +

These three chapters (*Why are We Afraid?*, *What Do You See?* and *On Death Beds*) challenge us to see ourselves and others through God's view of life and death!

(See pages 90-91 for additional personal and/or group study of Chapter Eight.)

POSTLUDE

I have been told "writing never ends," but for now my writing comes to an end.

My hope is that you have been encouraged and inspired by the intertwining of stories of how God revealed Himself as recorded in the Scriptures and stories of how He has revealed Himself to me. My hope is that you have been challenged by the honest questions within these pages.

Early in the Scriptures, we have the account of God revealing Himself to an Egyptian maidservant, Hagar. In Genesis 16:13, Hagar responds, "'You are the God who sees me.'" The Bible is filled with the written accounts of the God of the Bible revealing Himself to men, women, boys, girls, saints and sinners.

God has not changed! He continues to reveal Himself and probably has already revealed Himself to you!

My hope is that, through these Scriptures and stories, you will come to know "The God who sees you." God is ***amazing!***

In closing, "God is powerful, and there is something He has for you to do!"

I am sitting on the edge of what remains of the old swimming pool in Orleans, Nebraska. This is the spot where I sat 60 years ago after thinking I was going to drown.

I am walking to the pool house, now in disrepair, toward which I was walking 60 years ago when I heard a voice say, "God is powerful, and there is something He has for you to do!"

THE FOLLOWING SECTION IS INTENDED FOR YOUR PERSONAL STUDY OR THAT OF A SMALL GROUP

Chapter One

SEEING GOD'S HAND
(pages 1-10)

When does God begin to encounter a person?

There are four key questions about this experience:

1. Was it God's hand that I saw?

2. Was it God's voice that I heard?

3. What did God want me to do?

4. Why did this happen to me?

Do you believe this experience happened?

What do you know about God's right hand?
    (Exodus 15:6; Psalm 44:3; Matthew 26:64; Acts 7:55)

What do you know about angels?
    (Matthew 1:20; Luke 2:10; Acts 10:3-7)

The message to me had two parts:

1. "God is powerful,"
2. "and there is something He has for you to do!"

What is important about these two parts of the message?

What do these two parts of the message tell us about God?

What do the two parts of the message say to you?

Which of these points speak to you?

- God is not surprised by our difficulties.
- God knows people who feel insignificant.
- God is always closer than we realize.
- God uses bad times to get our attention.
- God brings the wonderful out of the horrible.
- God is powerful, but He still needs us.

Concluding points:

- God knew I would need this experience.
- God gives us stories to help others.
- God has given stories to many.

Do you have a story to tell?

Chapter Two

LEARNING TO WATCH FOR GOD
(pages 11-18)

In what ways have you learned to watch for God?

- in sickness?
- in catastrophes?
- in car accidents?
- in times of desperate prayer?
- other?

The Bible is filled with stories of God revealing Himself to people.

Exodus 3:12 — God to Moses
Joshua 1:5 — God to Joshua
Matthew 28:20 — Jesus to the disciples

What does it mean to say "God's Presence?"

What was the tabernacle?

Exodus 25:8

Exodus 25:30 (and Leviticus 24:5-9)

Exodus 25:31 (and Exodus 27:20-21)

David describes God's presence:

Psalm 31:20
Psalm 41:12
Psalm 89:15
Psalm 139:7

The truth of God's presence:

Matthew 1:23
John 1:14
John 14:17
Revelation 21:3

Consider the analogy of the stars referred to on page 14. Stars are always "present," but we only see them in the dark.

- Is God always there?

- Do we see God better in dark times?

Consider your prayer life:

- Do you pray for God to "show up" or do you pray believing He is always with you?

Why does God desire to live with us?

Chapter Three

GOD REVEALS HIMSELF TO US
(pages 19-30)

Consider how God reveals Himself to people in the Bible. How did God reveal Himself to these people?

Genesis 12:1 — Abram

Genesis 16:7 — Hagar

Exodus 3:4 — Moses

1 Samuel 3:4 — the boy Samuel

Matthew 1:20 — Joseph

Luke 1:26-27 — Mary

Acts 12:7 — Peter

Consider the comment on page 19 that the God of the Bible reveals Himself to male and female, young and old.

Consider the comment on page 20 that God knows your situation.

Three questions:

1. Does God reveal Himself only once to a person or many times?

    (Look at the story of Gideon in Judges 6:12 - Judges 7:10.)

2. Why does God reveal Himself to us?

    (Look at the story of Joseph in Genesis 50:20.)

3. Does God reveal Himself to all people?

    (Look at the story of the woman at the well in John 4.)

Has God revealed Himself to you?

Chapter Four

IMPORTANT POINTS TO REVIEW — I
(pages 31-34)

Reviewing:

- SEEING GOD'S HAND

- LEARNING TO WATCH FOR GOD

- GOD REVEALS HIMSELF

Do you agree that God uses hard times in our lives for the good? Why or why not?

Do you agree that it usually takes the dark times of life for us to see God? Why or why not?

Do you believe God is always with us? Why or why not?

If so, can this belief transform our prayer lives?

Do you agree that God speaks to us many times throughout our lives? Why or why not?

Do you agree that God reveals Himself to us for the purpose of saving many lives? Why or why not?

Do you agree that God reveals Himself to us during the ordinary activities of life? Why or why not?

Are your eyes open to seeing God around you?

Chapter Five

WHY ARE WE AFRAID?
(pages 35-40)

Consider this question asked on page 35:

Why do we still walk in the shadows of a life of <u>fear</u>, <u>doubt</u>, <u>worry</u> and <u>discouragement</u>?

Do you walk in the shadow of any of the above four?

Look at:

- God and Moses in Exodus 3 -4
  Why is Moses afraid?

- Jesus and the disciples in Matthew 14
  Why are the disciples afraid?

- Paul's last letter to Timothy in 2 Timothy: 1-4
  Why is Timothy struggling?

Did God ever give up on Moses?

Did Jesus ever give up on the disciples?

Did Paul ever give up on Timothy?

Has God ever given up on you?

Consider how to have victory over <u>fear</u>, <u>doubt</u>, <u>worry</u> and <u>discouragement</u> (page 39).

Acts 2:42 says to be devoted:

- To the teaching

- To the fellowship

- To the breaking of bread

- To prayer

The rest is left to God!

Is there a step you need to take? Teaching? Fellowship? Breaking of Bread? Prayer?

Chapter Six

WHAT DO YOU SEE?
(pages 41-56)

Questions:

- What do you see when you meet someone?

- What did Jesus see when he met someone?

- What do you see when you see yourself?

- What does Jesus see when he sees you?

Study Genesis 1:27

Dig deep into this verse! What does it mean?

Consider the Bible stories shared on pages 43-48.

The Woman at the Well	John 4:7
Mary Magdalene	Luke 8:2
Zacchaeus	Luke 19:1-4
Peter	Matthew 4:18

What do all these stories have in common?

How did Jesus see these people?

Do you see people like Jesus sees people?

Can you learn to see people like Jesus sees people?

What will happen in your life if you can see people like Jesus sees people?

What will happen in your life if you can see yourself like Jesus sees you?

Consider (as noted on page 53) that not all stories have a happy ending.

King Saul	1 Samuel 15:11
Young man	Matthew 19:21-22
Demas	2 Timothy 4:10

So, open your eyes — and look into the eyes of every man, woman and child you encounter.

Chapter Seven

ON DEATH BEDS
(pages 57-66)

Have you ever been with someone as they were dying?

What is happening when people are in the process of dying?

Consider the stories shared on pages 57-65.

Floyd
Captain Porter
Pearl
Arlie
Everett
Linda
Pauline
Randy

What do you learn about death and dying from these stories?

What do you learn about God from these stories?

How might this chapter help you when you are with someone who is dying?

How might this chapter help you as you approach your own death?

Reflect on this verse cited on page 65:

Psalm 23:4
Even though I walk through the darkest valley
[the valley of the shadow of death] ...
you are with me

Chapter Eight

IMPORTANT POINTS TO REVIEW — II
(pages 67-70)

Reviewing:

- WHY ARE WE AFRAID?

- WHAT DO YOU SEE?

- ON DEATH BEDS

Which of these three chapters spoke most directly to you?

Why?

Respond to the comment that all three chapters speak to one key point about the heart of God — God's eternal love for mankind.

Do you agree with that comment? Why or why not?

Consider Jonah (page 67) in Jonah 1-4.

- Who was he?

- What did God want him to do?

- Did Jonah want to do it?

- Jonah becomes angry with God in Jonah 4:7. Why?

- Why was God concerned about the people and animals of Nineveh?

Remember to see yourself and others through God's view of life and death.

GOD IS POWERFUL

THE
FOLLOWING
SECTION
INCLUDES
BONUS
INSIGHTS
INTENDED TO
BLESS YOU

BONUS INSIGHTS

What sustains us in our Christian journey? It is my joy to share with you two things that have sustained me.

ONE: I do some stretches and exercises every morning. I adapted one of my exercises, my sit-ups, to include the repetition of a verse of Scripture. Rather than counting to ten, I repeat a verse. Knowing that it is difficult for me to memorize verses, I use this as a way to strengthen my body, mind and soul. Here are the verses.

1. "Love the LORD your God with all your heart and with all your soul and with all your strength" (Deuteronomy 6:5). — *Moses*

2. "'Love your neighbor as yourself'" (Matthew 22:39). — *Jesus*

3. "Create in me a pure heart, O God, and renew a steadfast spirit within me" (Psalm 51:10). — *David*

4. "Trust in the LORD with all your heart and lean not on your own understanding; in all your ways submit to [acknowledge] him, and he will make your paths straight" (Proverbs 3:5-6). — *Solomon*

5. "'seek first his kingdom and his righteousness, and all these things will be given to you as well" (Matthew 6:33) — *Jesus*

6. "I urge you, brothers [and sisters], in view of God's mercy, to offer your bodies as a living sacrifice,

holy and pleasing to God—this is your true and proper worship" (Romans 12:1). — *Paul*

7. "'Come to me, all you who are weary and burdened, and I will give you rest'" (Matthew 11:28). — *Jesus*

<u>TWO</u>: As I struggled with wanting to have a balanced prayer life, one of the older ladies of the church taught me this acronym. This has guided my daily prayer life.

A — words of adoration to God and Jesus
C — confession of my sins and failures
T — thanking God for His acts of kindness
S — supplication or asking for help with the concerns of my life

ACKNOWLEDGEMENTS

As one who never expected to write a book, I must acknowledge those who encouraged me to write. They have helped me cross a bridge that I never expected to cross.

Special acknowledgement to Val Gwin. Her ability to edit my writing and to guide my efforts to publication of this book have been invaluable.

Special thanks to Pastor Sean Daugherty for his help in reviewing my writing. I thank God for him and his family and their faithfulness to God's calling on their lives.

Special thanks to Robin Stoops, former Executive Minister of ABC/NE and currently Associate General Secretary of ABCUSA, for his helpful comments.

Special thanks to William Bolen for providing the pictures of me sitting on the edge of the old swimming pool and walking to the old pool house—the places where my journey began.

And a very special thank you to my wife, Pam, for helping bring this project to fruition by reading several revisions, offering input and designing the cover of the book.

ORDER/DONATION INFORMATION

This book is provided to you at no cost.

In lieu of payment for this book and any subsequent copies, your donation to one of the following charitable Christ-centered organizations or to your church's benevolence fund will be appreciated.

> First Baptist Church
> 3610 6th Ave, Suite 1
> Kearney, NE 68845
> > (Please write "Deacon's Fund" in the memo section of your check.)

> Samaritan's Purse
> PO Box 3000
> Boone, NC 28607

If this book has blessed you, I ask you to consider doing two things:

1. Request additional copies for your family, friends or small study group.

2. Advertise this book on your social media sites so others can be aware of it and also be blessed.

For additional complimentary copies, please contact Stan Murdoch at

murdochstan51@gmail.com